Rhyme 'n' Reason

All rights reserved.

No part of this publication may be reproduced, stored in a retrieval system, or transmitted, in any form or by any means, electronic, mechanical, photocopying, recording or otherwise, without the prior written permission of the presenters.

Kirsty-ann Johnstone asserts the moral right to be identified as author of this work.

Presentation by *BookLeaf Publishing*

Web: www.bookleafpub.com

E-mail: info@bookleafpub.com

ISBN: 9789395223126

First edition 2022

DEDICATION

Dedicated to all those who despite their challenges, find a way to keep going and overcome them one step at a time.

ACKNOWLEDGEMENT

To my mum Janine Johnstone for always picking me up when times have been tough.
Plymouth Military Wives Choir for always giving me the encouragement to carry on.
Mike, Rob & Aj - what would I do without you dear friends.
To everyone who has given me support over the years, family, friends and of course vital charities The Baton, SSAFA and FND Action - I thank you

PREFACE

There is always someone who can relate to your situation and it's hoped you may just find something within this book that makes you feel you are not alone.

What the FND is this

You won't see me coming
I can suddenly appear
My presence hits you like a brick
And fills your head with fear

You won't know my next move
You'll feel every problem I make
You will feel so isolated
Your confidence, I'll take

I can come and go as I please
Without giving prior warning
I will tear apart the life you lived
And leave you in a state of mourning

You'll try to fight against me
And sometimes you will win
Other days I will consume you
Your will to try wearing thin

I'll take the strength from your limbs
Your skin will feel like it's crawling
I'll take over your balance
You can't control the falling

You will feel so overwhelmed
I'll be stopping you from sleeping
Your whole being exhausted
I may even stop you speaking

I will alter your memory
You'll struggle to understand
Your brain and body at war
And I am in command

I have no person preference
There is no hiding from me
I'm disrupting all your functions
Who am I? I'm FND

Progression

When you feel like you've hit rock bottom
There's only one way to go
Keep climbing over those hurdles
Eventually your strength will show

You can only do your best
A little more each day
Have faith, you'll get there
Keep those demons at bay

It can feel like an endless battle
One, with strength you'll face
It doesn't matter how long it takes
This isn't a race

You may progress quickly
You may progress a little slow
The point is you're moving forward
Allowing yourself to grow

Ride the Wave

Brain like the sea
Thoughts crashing into the caves
What you see on the surface
Is only the tip of the waves

Some disabilities are undercurrents
Until you're in them, you cannot know
They can drag you into an unknown place
Forced to go with their flow

No matter how hard you swim
You feel like you'll drown
Until a sense of calm surrounds you
No longer pulling you down

You keep treading water
Gasping for the air
You reach for the strength you need
It's within you, somewhere

The undercurrents are always there
Beneath the tide, they lie
But when you ride upon that wave
You'll feel like you can fly

Because of you

Most of the time I felt invisible
Walking, my head hanging low
My hair covering my face
So my tears did not show

I tripped over my shoelace
My bag fell to the floor
You were coming towards me
I didn't want to be there anymore

As you stepped a little closer
You offered me your hand
You broke away from the bullies
And decided to make a stand

To stand up for the vulnerable
To support the little guy
You changed my life in that moment
The day I wanted to die

Each day, I'd dread my day
When the bullies would appear
My world would start closing in
My insides shaking with fear

You saw me, no longer invisible
You'd shown me what kindness could do
I didn't have to spend days alone
You stood up, spoke out and I'm here because of you

Face the Day

Tomorrow is never given
For that, I'm truly sure
You cannot control the future
Or what challenges you'll endure

But you'll face each challenge
Just as you have before
One step at a time
Until you achieve a little more

Some days will be harder than others
Those are the days you fight
You fight for what you truly deserve
In the dark, seek out the light

You can achieve anything
You may have to adapt your ways
This is the production of your life
You control how it plays

If you have to revisit a scene
That is okay too
Just don't pause there too long
Keep on pushing through

Unmasked

Why do you wear this mask?
The one saying "I'm okay"
How I wish you'd have the courage
Find the strength to walk away

The door may seem far away
A barrier to the unknown
A feeling of familiarity
Being simpler than living alone

But then you take another blow
How did it get this far?
Please find the opportunity
To pack, get in that car

Let the tears fall down your face
Have faith, you will cope
Look towards that open road
It's a beacon of hope

You can be safe, back in control
Tell loved ones how you feel
No need for the mask anymore
They'll help you rebuild and heal

Through the Lens

A complete sense of calm
Patiently waiting for the shot
A swan gracefully opens its wings
A few clicks and it's caught

The perfectly timed moment
With ample amount of light
The heron poses on a rock
Preparing for its flight

The ripples on the lake
A duckling swimming near
A quick check of the shutter speed
Ensuring the feathers are crystal clear

Respecting the surroundings
Peace and beauty at its best
Memories now captured
Let nature rest

Taking notice

Do you see me?
I've been struggling for a while
I see you from the window
And I always raise a smile

There you go again
Rushing in every way
I'd come out to my door
But what would I say?

Hello, I'm your neighbour
Lived here twenty years
Could I trouble you for help?
Until I get over my fears

I had a fall not so long ago
I'm scared to leave my home
I don't have any support
And live here on my own

But why would I trouble you?
You don't even know my name
Not enough time in your day
Your routine always the same

But I'll keep smiling from my window
Reminded of how my life used to be
And maybe you'll stop for a moment
You might just see me

Talking to the wall

What is Isolation like?
Well, the rooms are very small
I've turned into Shirley Valentine
Yes, I'm talking to the wall

The cat isn't one for conversation
He goes out more than me
I greet delivery drivers like celebrities
As they drop ingredients for my tea

I see the postman daily
Who must wonder if I own any clothes
Not that I answer the door naked
Just whatever pyjamas I chose

Doing washing is a bit of excitement
I might even do an extra spin
That'll take an extra ten minutes
Time to pour the gin

Weekends in are the new going out
Except the bar quickly depletes
No table service in these four walls
No disco lights or party beats

Nope, Isolation is pretty dull
Especially alone with a cat
The only thing that changes
Is the waistline, I'm getting fat

But alas, Joe Wicks appears
And saves my bursting jeans
One more squat will do it
Before I tackle the custard creams

Who really cares anyway?
No judgement here after all
Just me and the sleeping cat
Getting advice from a wall

Time

As time passes
Never have regrets
Say all you need to say
Before the sun sets

As time passes
Do things which make you smile
Don't waste a moment
Saying "I'll do it in a while"

The clock is ticking
Your dreams won't wait
Your vision of life awaits you
Try and not be late

As time passes
Make every second count
Your life could be filled with riches
Don't settle for a discount

Love and be loved
For exactly as you are
Accept and be accepted
For every flaw and scar

Don't delay your happiness
Life will simply pass you by
Time will go so quickly
It's time for you to fly

Days like these

Some days
I have an overwhelming rage inside
Some days
I just want to crawl into a hole and hide
Some days
I feel guilty about the things I cannot do
Some days
An achievement is putting on a shoe
Some days
I manage to raise a smile
Some days
I just need to cry for a while
Some days
I melt into my family's embrace
Some days
I'm isolated and feel out of place
Some days
I'm motivated and go for a walk
Some days
I've no energy and struggle to talk
Other days
I feel the hours just passing me by
These are the days I'm left contemplating why
Why has life given this journey to me?
Is it a lesson I cannot see?

This body I'm in, now feels strange
I must adapt, It requires a change
Each day
I must do everything I can
I am still who I was
I'm just following a different plan

Planting Roots

Life can be a rocky road
But you can still enjoy the road
Just don't focus on the bumps
Look around, see nature thrive

The autumnal leaves
Creating an archway of gold
Flourishing with clear direction
Even when they seem uncontrolled

The purplest of heather
Grows in the toughest terrain
With strength in its roots
It's beautiful, even in rain

The history of a building will remain
Even when the ruins have been forecast
The green from the fragile moss
Shields the foundations from its past

Everything has its place in time
Adapting to the environment around
Growing and embracing change
Roots firmly in the ground

Sacrifice

Every poppy represents a soul
Of all who played a vital role
In the days years ago
Heroes lie, crosses row on row

Those who paid the ultimate sacrifice
All those who saved a life
Carrying a comrade upon their shoulder
As the night fell and the air grew colder

Those who fought on with an internal flame
Knowing life would never be the same
A burning strength within their core
As the final blow took them to the floor

Laid on the ground, bloody and alone
Thoughts drifting back to home
Warm tears crawl from the eye
As they gave their final sigh

We may not know all your names
But we live the days you cannot
We remember the future is ours
Because of the days you fought

To you, a hero, a friend
For the service you gave, a toast
In the distance a bugle calls
This is your last post

Survivor

Look at me now
There's no uniform I wear
No shoes upon my feet
No need, bound in a wheelchair

I served my country
Who could have known?
It could have been any one of us
When that IED was blown

They were just gone
Nothing there below the knee
In an instant, life changed
Nobody just saw me

Life has carried on
Although the struggle is real
I cannot begin to explain
How the phantom pains feel

I'm not the same person I was
But I'm stronger than before
That day may have taken my legs
Disabled? I'm so much more

Broken Veteran

Staring at the box of pills
I wonder how long it'd take
For me to just drift away
No more decisions to make

My thoughts are destructive
Loneliness fills my day
Nights I'm filled with fear

I've really lost my way
I ran into personal struggles
Then I lost my home
Existing in a doorway
Within the dirty streets I roam

I don't take drugs
Alcohol takes off the edge
I'm a homeless veteran
Balancing on a ledge

Once I left the service
Nobody supported me
My relationships deteriorated
Diagnosed with PTSD

I miss the person I was
I'm not him anymore
All I ask is for understanding
As I lie here on the floor

So next time you walk past
Don't look at me and sneer
Ask yourself if more could have been done
To keep me from being here

I don't want to be this way
I'm doing all I can
To find the person I was before
I'm just a broken man

Judgement

I hate the way you look at me
And jeer as I'm walking past
Venomous hatred from your mouth
Sadness is what you cast

You may not like how I look
You may not see the beauty in my face
But who are you to judge me?
Your hatred has no place

There is no perfection within this world
Differences affect us all
Abilities, sexuality, race, religion
Plump, thin, short or tall

Words can wound the recipient
And have a detrimental effect
If this was someone you knew
You'd naturally protect

These things do not define us
It's the people we are inside
No two flowers are the same
Yet will bloom side by side

Self Love

Today is the day
I love myself in every way
All the imperfections are part of me
Every scar and every wrinkle I see
Even the scars hidden away
Make me the person I am today
I'm a survivor of chapters past
A warrior fighting each challenge cast
I cannot change what has gone
But there's a blank page with each new dawn
Trivial things no longer at the fore
It's the simplest things I want more
All the things I've had no confidence to do
This is for me, not for you
My inner happiness must be met
Not spending days with regret
I will love myself in every way
Today is the day

The Mother in me

I knew I could love you
But it wasn't meant to be
I knew I'd be a good mother
Body lacking physically

I dreamt of you long before
Of how our life would be
How we'd play in the park
Or you climbing your first tree

I imagined you at school
Waving our first goodbye
You not winning your races
And me telling you it was more important to try

You'd be spoilt by grandma
Unable to resist your big blue eyes
And I knew how much she'd love you
And how she'd soothe your cries

I had imagined your wedding
What song would play for your first dance
Oh, I would have loved that moment
If I'd only had the chance

Each Mother's Day that passes
I'm always left wondering why
Why I would never hold you
Or hear your first cry

I have a sense of emptiness
That you were never meant to be
I grieve you were never born
That's just the mother in me

The Unexpected Child

You never grew within me
But you grew within my heart
I loved you with all my being
Right from the very start

I was proud to be your stepmum
Cherished every school play
Loved our little memories
Treasured in every way

I gave you everything I had
But you gave me more
You filled the emptiness
I could no longer ignore

I'd never be called mum
But you made me whole
I'd give you the love I'd been given
That was my sincerest goal

I'm proud of who you are
I love how you've grown
I wish you the happiness you gave to me
And you pass on the love you were shown

Dear Future Self

Dear future self
Look at what you've gone through
Process those moments in your life
And just be proud of you

You battled over hurdles
You adapted and overcame
You moved forward
Without assigning blame

You never stopped for a moment
To really adjust your sails
Then the wind caught up with you
And spun you with its gales

But you stood firm
You fought and achieved
Determined to move forward
In you, you believed

Dear future self
It's time for a different view
You're stronger than you thought
Just love being you

Breathe

Breathe in, Breathe out
Feel your chest as it expands
Stretch your arms fully
All the way to your hands

Roll your head to the left
Then roll it to the right
Roll your shoulders backward
Stop your muscles feeling tight

Deep breathing
Count In 1,2,3 out 4,3,2,1
Just be in the moment
Surrounded by no-one

Take yourself to a place
Only your mind can go
It's peaceful and tranquil
Let these positive thoughts flow

You are capable of anything
You deserve good things
Take this time, carry it forward
Embracing all that peace brings